ADAPTIVE

SPORTS

FUNDAMENTALS

ADAPTIVE

SPORTS

FUNDAMENTALS

Fundamental skills of:
Basketball, Football, Soccer, Baseball,
Badminton, Track, Volleyball, Softball,
Ultimate Frisbee & Tennis.

A step-by-step guide for teaching children and young adults the fundamental skills of 10 of the most popular sports.

RICARDO A. CUNNINGHAM

Table of Contents

Introduction

Many children learning to play sports today have not developed the fundamental skills of the sport in order to play the proper way. Learning the fundamental skills is very important for children to be successful at their particular sport of choice. It is the basic foundation they need to know when they are learning to play any sport. Fundamentals will help the child to be a more superior athlete and versatile in their athletic skills. Many of the fundamental skills can be adapted to several different sports. When you develop all the fundamentals skills it makes all the other related skills easy to develop. Learning the core skills will also help to minimize injures and the child will enjoy playing more as they advance their athleticism. Many children are injured in sports because they have not developed the proper fundamental skills and the appropriate technique to play. To avoid injuries, it is important to learn the fundamental skills of the sport. Mastering the fundamental skills will extend the child's longevity in that particular sport; it will help the child to play with more self-confidence, empower the child to participate more and take more chance when he/she is playing. Once the child develops all the fundamental skills, he/she must have acquired a lifetime of skills.

In 2011, I started a children's adaptive fitness center, LCF Kids, formerly known as Life Changing Fitness. This company was founded because of my passion for helping children to develop their gross motor skills and motor planning skills, so that they are able to perform physical activities and sports at a high level. We teach children and young adults the fundamental skills of all sports and help them to enhance their motor planning skills.

I participated in competitive sports for over 25 years, and taught physical education for over a decade. I was a full scholarship athlete in track and field for five years during college. Since then, it has been my mission and passion to help every child to develop their fundamental skills regardless of their skill level and abilities. I believe this is my purpose in life, to give every child the opportunity to participant in physical movement. At my facilities, we use innovative equipment to make exercise fun for the children as they learn the skills. We use adaptive and hands-on techniques for those children that have difficulty learning the traditional way and need more assistance. This gives us the ability to modify the skills based on the participant's individual needs. It is best to start out teaching the skills and catering for the child's strength. Once the child develops his/her basic skills, we move on to more difficult skills to build self-confidence.

Over the years, parents have always asked me to focus on teaching their children sports fundamental skills. They knew how important these skills are for their children's development regardless of their ability to move and coordinate their body efficiently. So, I realized the need to get this book on the market. There is no other book currently out that breaks down the techniques step by step on how to perform the skills.

As I explain the steps for the different sports, please remember to first adhere to the safety precautions of each sport. It is vital to know that safety is a priority in sports. Participants should also remember to wear the appropriate clothing for the sport and to stay properly hydrated. I also stated some of the basic rules of the game. This is not a complete list of all the rules as those could be very extensive. The rules mentioned in this book are at a lower level for the participants learning the basic fundamental skills. For participants at a competitive level, the rules of the specific sport can be found on the National leagues website.

Learning Styles

For us to learn, we depend on our senses to process the information around us. The three main learning styles are: visual learning, auditory learning and kinesthetic learning. Everyone has one learning style that may be more effective than the others. It is very important to apply the right style of learning when teaching children. When you apply the style of learning that best suits the child, the child will be more motivated because they are able to process the information faster. And they are able to absorb the material easier. Applying the right style will also build their confidence and self-esteem.

Visual Learning

A visual learner is someone that learns best by *seeing* how something is done. They are able to retain the information and repeat what was done.

Auditory Learning

An auditory learner is someone that learns best by *listening* to directions and instructions given to them.

Kinesthetic Learning

A kinesthetic learner is someone that learns best through *hands-on experience.* The instructor needs to hold their hands and take them through the motion of the activity.

It is important that you know how to apply the learning styles when teaching the participant. When you begin working with the participant, you should apply all three styles of learning to see which style works best. Once you know the best fit for the participant, you should use that as your primary technique of teaching them.

You should note that some activities may require a different style of learning for the participant. You may need to apply multiple styles on occasions. For example, the participant may be a visual learner as a primary style, but when the participant is learning how to bat you may need to apply both visual techniques and kinesthetic techniques. In my experience working with children over the last fourteen years, I have found that over 95% of children that are challenged with these skills absorb the information and learn faster when you apply the visual and kinesthetic learning techniques.

Chapter 1

Basketball

Safety Precaution:

❖ Participants should dress appropriately, wear proper basketball short and shirt to move easily, as well as wear proper basketball footwear and socks to minimize ankle sprain and prevent sliding during fundamental skills acquisition.

❖ Skills should be performed in a big open space. Ensure that the surface is not wet or have cracks to avoid injuries.

❖ Make sure that participants are paying attention and keep their eyes on the ball at all times.

❖ Remind participants to minimize the ball from hitting them in the head or face.

❖ During shooting skills, ensure that participants are not too close to the basketball rim. They should have sufficient space to react and catch the ball if it hits the rim.

- ❖ During catching skills, participants should place their hands in front of their chest not their face, to minimize head and face injuries
- ❖ Participants should relax their hands so that fingers are relaxed during catching and dribbling, to minimize finger injuries.

Basic Rules:

- ❖ Five (5) players on each team.
- ❖ Court positions are: Center (position near the basket), Offense (position in an open and get the ball or shoot the basket), Defense (position near the opponent to prevent them from shooting or blocking their shot), Forward (position in the far corner of the court to receive the ball), and Guard (passes the ball to the offensive player)
- ❖ Points: 1pt (free throw), 2pt (inside three point line), 3pt (behind the three point line).
- ❖ No travelling- players are not allowed to run with the ball.
- ❖ No double dribbling- players are not allowed to bounce the ball using both hand simultaneously.
- ❖ No carrying – players are not allowed to place their hands under the ball or too far to the side.

Hands must remain at the top of the ball when dribbling.

Basketball is a great team sport that is played between two teams of five players each. The objective of the game is to score goals through the basketball ball hoop. Basketball helps to build team work, and social skills through play. It helps to improve coordination, agility, strength and stamina. Basketball consists of four main skills: passing, dribbling, shooting, and layups.

Passing

Passing is one of the fundamental skills of playing basketball. Players move the ball up and down the court through passing. It's the great way to get all the players involved during the games. There are three type of passing: chest passing, bounce passing and overhead passing.

Chest passing is a very important skill when you are playing basketball. Players use chest passing to share the ball with their team members. Here are the steps needed to perform chest passing:

1. Participant should place the ball below their chin to the center of their chest.
2. Position their hands by placing them to the sides of the ball.
3. Place their arms with elbows pointing outward to the side of the body.
4. Step forward with non-dominant leg and knees slightly bent.
5. Push the ball forward by extending their arms from the chest to release the ball and follow through.
6. Do a minimum of three sets of 20, for three to five times per week for repetition and consistency.

Figure 1: Proper position for basketball chest pass

Adaptive chest passing (hands-on-technique)

If the participant is having difficulty following the steps above, you should follow the adaptive or hands-on technique:

1. Visually demonstrate all the steps for doing a chest pass.
2. Place two poly spots on the floor, one in front of the other, two inches apart.
3. The participant should stand on one poly spot.
4. Stand close to the participant so that you can assist with all the steps.
5. Help the participant to place the ball in front of their chest with fingers spread apart (the ball should not touch their body).
6. Assist the participant with stepping forward to the other poly spot by placing your hands on their, non-dominant, lower leg to help them step onto the poly spot with their knees lightly bent
7. Stand behind the participants and assist them by holding their lower arms and helping them to push the ball forward by extending their arms out from their chest to release the ball and follow through.
8. Do at least three scts of 20 repetitions, three to five times per week
9. Give a two minute break between sets if the participant gets frustrated or loses focus.

Bounce passing is another type of passing when passing the ball to team members, by bouncing the ball to each other. The skills you need to perform bounce passing are as follow:

1. Position the ball at the center of the participant's chest (ball should not touch their body).
2. Place their arms in an upright position with the elbows pointing to the side.
3. Step forward with the non-dominant leg and knees slightly bent.
4. Push the ball from the chest outward to the ground by extending the arms out and following through.
5. Do at least three sets of 20, three to five times per week.

Figure 2: Proper position for basketball bounce pass

Adaptive Bounce Passing

1. Demonstrate visually how to perform the skills.

2. Place two poly spots on the ground directly in front of each other, two inches apart.

3. The participant should stand on one spot and step forward on the other spot. Adjust the spacing between spots based on the height of the participant.

4. Assist the participant with standing correctly with legs apart and placing the ball in front of their chest.

5. Stand in front of the participant and direct them to place their dominant foot on the spot.

6. Assist the participant with stepping forward onto the other spot by placing your hand on their lower leg to step forward and both knees slightly bent.

7. Stand behind the participant to assist with pushing the ball forward by holding the participant's lower arms and having them push the ball outward from their chest to the ground, then release the ball and follow through.

8. Do a minimum of three sets of 15, three to five times per week.

If the participant becomes frustrated or is having difficulty staying focused, give two minute breaks between sets.

Overhead passing

Here are the steps to perform overhead passing.

1. Participant should stand with legs apart.
2. Holding the ball with both hands, place the ball over their heads with elbows bent.
3. Step forward with the non-dominant leg slightly bent.
4. Pass the ball by extending their arms out from over their head then release the ball and follow through.
5. Do a minimum of three sets of 30 repetitions, three to five times per week.

Adaptive overhead passing

1. Demonstrate how to perform the skills visually.
2. Place two poly spots directly in front of each other and two inches apart, adjust the distance of the spot according to the participant's height
3. Stand beside the participant to assist with standing with legs apart and the ball placed above their heads and elbows bent.

4. Assist the participant by directing them to step with the non-dominant leg and knees slightly bent.

5. Switch positions to standing behind the participant to assist with passing the ball forward.

6. Hold the participant's lower arm to help them move their arms forward by extending their arms outward to release the ball and follow through.

7. Do at least three set of 20, three to five times per week.

   If the participant gets frustrated or has difficulty staying focused, give two minute breaks between sets.

Dribbling

Dribbling is one of the main skills required to move the ball up the court. Dribbling helps to build ball control, hand eye coordination, and visual spatial awareness. Here are the skills to perform dribbling:

1. Stand in the correct position with legs apart, knees slightly bent and back in an upward position.

2. Place the dominant hand in the position of a downward arc at waist height and fingers pointing down.

3. The non-dominant hand should be extended and slightly bent to protect the ball as they dribble.

4. Push the ball downwards from the waist to the ground, with fingers pointing down.

5. Continue the back and forth motion, keep the head up during the process.

6. Do a minimum of three set of 30 with each hand, three to five times per week.

Figure 5: Proper dribbling form

Adaptive Dribbling

1. Demonstrate visually how to perform the skills.
2. Place two poly spots on the ground for the participant to stand on.
3. Have the participant stand with knees bent and their back in an upright position.
4. Start with stationary dribbling first. Stand behind the participant and place your hand over their dominant hand.
5. Have the participant push the ball with their hand in shape of downward arc, from their waist to the ground, and keep their knees slightly bent
6. Continue this back and forth, and perform 15 dribbles with each hand.
7. Do at least three sets of 15 dribbles of each hand, three to five times per week.
8. Break sets in half if the participant start to get frustrated or have difficulty staying focused.

If the participant gets frustrated or has difficulty remaining focused, give two minute breaks between sets.

Shooting

Shooting is extremely important to playing the game. The outcome of the game is determined by how accurate or consistent you are when you are shooting the basketball. The steps to perform these skills are as follow:

1. The participant should stand with space between both legs.
2. Position their arms by placing their shooting hand under the ball with fingers spread apart.
3. Place the guiding hand at the side of the ball to help control the ball.
4. Bend the knees and arms, flex the wrist back, and extend the arms out.
5. Move the knees back into straight position with wrists flexed forward to release the ball.
6. Follow through with downward arc.
7. Do a minimum of three sets of 30, three to five times per week.

Figure 3: Position hands to shoot basketball

Adaptive Shooting Technique

1. Demonstrate visually how to perform the skills so that the participant can observe.

2. Place two poly spots close to each other for the participant to stand with knees slightly bent.

3. Place the ball in the shooting hand with wrist flexed backward and guiding hand on the side of the ball.

4. Stand behind the participant and place your hands over the participants' hands and assist with extending their arms straight to the basket, as their knees return to a straight position.

27

5. The shooting hand should follow through with down ward arc when the ball is released.

6. Do at least three sets of 20, three to five times per week.

7. If the children gets frustrated or has difficulty remaining focused, give two minute breaks between sets.

Figure 4: Proper form to shoot basketball

Layups

Layup is a key skill for scoring a basket during the basketball game. It's an easy way to score but difficult for younger participants. Layups require balancing, coordination and motor planning skills. Here are the steps to perform layups:

1. Dribble slowly to the side of the basket so that they can use the backboard to make the layup.
2. Jump using the opposite leg from the layup hand and extend your arms out to the basket.
3. Release the ball to the top of the arc of the backboard. Example if you are using your right hand to layup, you should jump with your left leg.

Figure 6: Proper form for basketball layup

Adaptive basketball layup

1. Demonstrate visually how to perform the layup.

2. Place two poly spots as a guide for the participant. One poly spot at the starting position and the other at the side of the basket so that they will know when to stop dribbling.

3. Have the participant dribble on the spot slowly to the backboard.

4. Once the participant gets close to the backboard, have the participant take two steps and jump using the opposite leg of the arm being used for the layup.

8. Layup the ball by extending their arms to the basket, then release by rolling the ball off their fingers, or shoot off the backboard (if they jump with their left foot they should layup with their right arm).

9. Do three sets of ten layups, three to five times per week.

If the children gets frustrated or has difficulty remaining focused, give two minute breaks between sets.

Chapter 2

FOOTBALL

Safety Precautions:

- ❖ Drills should be performed in an open space (preferably a grass field).
- ❖ Avoid extremely hot weather, and remain hydrated.
- ❖ All participants should wear proper safety helmet, football cleats, football gloves and pads.
- ❖ Participant should warm up for 10 minutes and stretch their body before performing these skills.
- ❖ Explain to the participants to always avoid head collisions to prevent concussions.
- ❖ Participants should position their hands below their chin and avoid placing hand in front of their face. This will minimize the ball from hitting the participant in the face during catching.
- ❖ Parents should use their judgment when performing throwing skills, avoid excess amounts of throwing in one day. This will minimize

shoulder injuries; I recommend 30-55min workout per day.

Rules:

- ❖ There are eleven players on each team: offensive players and defensive players.
- ❖ The offensive team with the football has four chances to complete a 10 yard pass to continue with the play. If they don't, the opposing team gets the ball.
- ❖ One touchdown is six points and a kick is one point.
- ❖ When tackling the opposing player, a player cannot grab the player's face mask.
- ❖ A player can ONLY tackle a player with the ball, or a player that is down.
- ❖ Players can't interfere with kicker or player who is receiving a pass.
- ❖ There should be NO helmet to helmet contact, to minimize injuries/concussion

Warm-ups & Stretches

Warm up drills include: running, jumping jacks or jump rope. Basic stretching include: touching knees or toes with both hands and holding it for 10 seconds and extended arms in to a straight position in front of your body and hold it for 15 seconds   (x3)

Football is a team sport played with 11 players on each team. The objective of the game is to get the ball across the opposing team's goal line into the end zone, which is called a touchdown. The fundamental skills needed to play football are as follow: throwing, catching, kicking/punting the ball, and caring the ball/running with the ball.

Throwing

Throwing a football is very essential to playing the game. The quarterback executes most of the throwing during the game. Throwing helps to improve upper body strength, midline movement and coordination. These are the steps necessary to perform throwing:

1. The participant should hold the football by placing their hand over the ball with fingers tightly gripped around the lace and the index finger pointed to the tip of the ball.
2. Stand with feet apart and knees slightly bent.
3. The non-dominant side of their body should be facing the throwing direction.

4. Extend the throwing arm outward with a slight bend behind the shoulder of the throwing arm and extend the other arm forward slightly bent.

5. Step forward with non-dominant leg and rotate the hips, shoulder and ankles in the direction you are throwing the ball.

6. Extend your throwing arm forward and release the ball.

7. Follow through after the ball is released with a downward arc.

8. Do three sets of 20 reps, three to five times per week.

Instructors may add more reps if the participant is able to do more without getting fatigued.

Figure 7: Proper way to hold the football

Adaptive Throwing (Hands on technique for throwing)

1. Demonstrate visually how to perform the skills
2. Place three spots on the ground five (5) inches apart in a straight line, one each for the right and left leg and the other spot to step onto when throwing.

3. Assist the participant with standing sideways with the non-dominant side facing the direction they are going to throw, with feet apart and knees slightly bent.

4. Assist the participant with holding the football by placing their hand over the ball with fingers tightly gripped around the lace and the index finger pointing to the tip of the ball.

5. Assist participant with positioning the throwing arm slightly bent above their shoulder, and the other hand extended forward.

6. Stand behind the participant and place your hand over the participant's lower leg to assist the participant with stepping forward onto the third poly spot, and rotating their hip and shoulder.

7. As they rotate their hip and shoulder, they extend the throwing arm to release the ball.

8. Follow through after the ball is released, with the throwing arm into downward arc.

9. Do three sets of 15 reps, three to five times per week.

Catching a football

Catching is the ability to secure the football from the air, and maintain full possession of the ball until the play is complete. Caching helps to improve eye-hand coordination, tracking and visual spatial awareness. Here are the steps to perform catching:

1. Stand with knees slightly bent.
2. Participant should be directly positioned in front of the ball when catching.
3. Position arms upright and slightly bent, with both hands close to each other in center of the chest.
4. Open hands fully in the shape of two half-moons facing each other, with space between them.
5. Extend arms forward in front of their body/in the direction of the ball, then secure the ball from the air with both hands.
6. Once the ball is caught, retract your arm to bring the ball back close to your body to secure the ball.
7. Maintain possession of the ball until the game is complete.
8. Do three sets of 20 reps, three to five times per week

Parents can add more reps if the participant is not fatigued or getting frustrated.

Figure 8: Proper form for catching a football

Adaptive Catching (Hands on technique)

1. Demonstrated visually how to perform the skills
2. Place two poly spot on the ground for the participant to stand on.
3. Assist the participant with standing in position with their knees slightly bent.

4. Assist the participant with placing their arms in an upright position with the center of their body and elbow slightly bent.

5. Stand behind the participant and place your hands on the participant's lower arm, helping them to extend their arms out in the direction of the ball then secure the ball from the air.

6. Once the ball is caught, retract arms close to the chest to keep the ball in possession until the play is complete.

7. Do three sets of 20 reps, three to five times per week

Parents can add more reps if the participant is not fatigued or getting frustrated

Chapter 3

SOCCER

Safety Precautions:

❖ Participants should wear proper soccer gears: comfortable soccer cleats, socks, shorts or sweat pants and short or long sleeve shirt.

❖ Do light warm ups and stretch to loosen the muscles.

❖ Drills should be performed in an open space on a grass field.

❖ Practice in the appropriate weather, avoid extremely hot weathers unless you are hydrated.

❖ Remind participants to use proper techniques such as using the side of their foot to kick the ball (not their toes) to avoid injuries.

❖ Minimize the ball from hitting participants in their head unless properly trained on how to perform passing using their head.

Rules:

❖ There are eleven (11) players on each team.

❖ Only the goalkeepers are allowed to use their hands to touch the ball.

❖ Positions: Offense (has the ball trying to score a goal), Defense (trying to block the opponent from scoring), mid field (play in the middle), wing players (players on the outer line of the field), goalkeeper (blocks the opponent from scoring).

❖ Scores: 1 goal is obtained by kicking the ball across the opposing team's goal line.

❖ Time: Two halves of 45 minutes each (90 min game).

❖ Fowls: Cannot kick, jump, trip, charge, strike, push, hold or spit on someone (results in yellow or red card).

❖ Penalty: Red card (automatically out of the game), Yellow card (warning).

Soccer is a team sport where two teams play against each other. Each team consist of eleven players, the objective of the game is to kick the soccer ball across the goal of the opponent. The only person allowed to touch the ball with their hand is the goalkeeper. The fundamental skills needed to play soccer are the following: kicking, dribbling, passing, and stopping the soccer ball.

Kicking

Soccer kicking is the most essential skill you need to play soccer; 95% of the game is played by kicking the ball. Kicking helps to improve: eye foot coordination, gross motor skills, midline, and lower leg strength. Here are the steps to perform soccer kicking:

1. Stand in position behind the ball with feet apart.

2. Step with the non-dominant foot to the side of the ball.

3. The dominant foot should be in the shape of the Letter L with your body in front of the ball.

4. Drive the dominant foot forward rotating the hips and shoulders, and kick the ball with the inner part of the foot.

5. Follow through with your leg across your body after you kick the ball.

6. Do three sets of 15 kicks, three to five times per week.

Figure 9: Starting position to kick a soccer ball

Adaptive kicking

1. Demonstrate visually how to perform the skills for the participant to observe.

1. Place three poly spots on the floor, three to five inches apart, in the shape of a triangle. (Adjust the distance between them based on the height of the participant).

2. Place the ball on one of the poly spots, have the child stand on another poly spot, place his/her

non-dominant foot on the last poly spot. The participant should not be stretching to reach the spots.

3. Place your hand on the outer side of the participant's dominant foot and propel the foot forward using the inner part of his/her foot to make contact with the ball.

4. Have the participant follow through across their body.

5. Do three sets of 20 kicks, three to five times per week

If the participant gets frustrated or loses interest in performing the skills, give two to three minute breaks between sets to keep them engaged.

Passing

Passing involves kicking the ball with the side of your foot to your team mate during a soccer game. Passing helps to build team work, communication and cooperation. The steps needed to perform passing are as follow:

1. Position the body behind the ball.
2. Step to the side of the ball with the non-dominant leg.
3. Place the dominant foot behind the ball with sufficient space and rotate the hip slightly.
4. Swing the foot and rotate your hip and shoulder at the same time to make contact with the ball and follow through after the kick.
5. Do three set of 20 passes, three to five times per week.

Adaptive passing

1. Demonstrate visually how to perform all the steps for the participant to follow.
2. Place three spots on the ground five inches apart from each other in the shape of a triangle.
3. Place the ball on one poly spot, assist the participant with positioning their body behind the ball on the other poly spot, with one foot at the side of the ball and the other foot behind the ball.
4. Place your hand on the participant's lower leg and help them to swing their leg forward and rotate your hip at the same time to pass the ball slowly to your teammates.

5. Do three set of 15 passes, three to five times per week.

If the participant gets frustrated or loses interest in performing the skills, give two to three minute breaks between   sets   to   keep   them   engaged.

Stopping

Stopping the ball is another key skill needed to play soccer. Stopping the ball helps to slow down the speed of the game and allow the players to set up plays. There are different ways to stop the ball such as using the legs, chest and head. The only person allowed to use his/her hands to stop the ball is the goal keeper. Here are the steps to perform to stop the ball:

1. Position the participant in front of the ball.
2. Lift the dominant leg off the ground and slightly move his/her foot forward towards the ball using the inner part of their foot.
3. Place the foot in front of the ball so that it can stop.
4. Either foot can be used to stop the ball.
5. Do three set of 20, three to five times per week.

Figure 10: Proper way to stop a soccer ball

Adaptive technique for stopping the ball

1. Demonstrate visually how to perform all the steps for the participant to observe.

2. Place two poly spots on the ground five inches apart from each other, for the participant to stand on with legs apart.

3. Assist the participant with standing on the spots.

4. Assist the participant with lifting their foot off the ground with the inner side facing the ball.

5. Have someone pass the ball directly to the participant.

6. Place your hand on the lower leg of the participants to help them move their foot in front of the ball to stop it.

7. Do three set of 15, three to five times per week.

If the participant gets frustrated or loses interest in performing the skills, give two to three minute breaks between sets to keep them engaged.

Chapter 4

BASEBALL

Safety Precaution:

- ❖ Participants should wear proper baseball gear such as: baseball helmet, baseball cleats, baseball gloves, bats, and balls.

- ❖ Baseball skills should bc performed in an open space on a grass or dirt field, preferably a baseball field.

- ❖ Participant should have full control of their bats as they make contact with ball. Remind participant to have a tight grip holding their bat and control their bat when they follow through across their body.

- ❖ Parents and coaches should be aware that the bat can slip during batting and should be careful at all times.

- ❖ Parents and coaches should have sufficient space between themselves and the participant.

❖ During throwing skills, ensure that the surrounding area is clear. Thrower should always give alert to the person the/she will toss the ball.

❖ Participants should place hands in the right position during catching skills, avoid placing hands in front of their faces and keep their eyes on the ball at all times.

Rules:

❖ There are nine players on a baseball team.

❖ There are nine innings in a professional game and in the youth, there is between six and seven innings

❖ If the batter misses the ball three times in a row, they strike out.

❖ The batter must run all bases in orderly manner.

❖ If a member of the opposing team gets the ball and throws it to the base before the batter returned to base they are out.

❖ When the batter runs to the first base, they receive a single, base two is a double, and base three is a triple.

❖ When the batter runs all three bases without stopping, they receive a homerun.

Baseball is a game that is played between two teams of nine players on the field. Baseball helps to build eye-hand coordination, midline, arm strength, upper-body strength and team work. There are four fundamental skills needed to play baseball: batting, pitching, catching, and fielding.

Batting a baseball

The steps needed to perform batting skills are:

1. The participant should stand sideways with their shoulder squared, feet apart, with the non-dominant leg facing the pitcher and dominant leg behind.
2. Hold the bat tightly with both hands close to each other.
3. Slightly bend their knees.
4. Position the arms (holding the bat) above the shoulders
5. Rotate the hips and shoulders and swing the arms forward across the body to make contact with the ball.
6. Follow through across the body after they make contact with ball.
7. Do three set of 20, three to five times per week.

Figure 11: Proper form for batting baseball

Parents or coaches can use their discretion to do more repetitions if the participant is capable of doing so without being fatigued or frustrated.

Adaptive Batting

1. Visually demonstrate how to perform all the steps for the participant to observe.

2. Place two poly spots five inches apart from each other.

3. Assist the participant with the proper stance: standing sideways with feet apart, the non-dominant leg in front and the dominant leg behind.

53

4. Hold the bat with both hands tightly gripped, and their knees slightly bent.

5. Assist the participant with positioning above their shoulders.

6. Stand behind the participant and place your hands over their lower arms to assist them with moving their arms forward, swinging the bat as they rotate their shoulder and hips toward the direction of the pitcher.

7. As the bat makes contact with the ball, the participant should follow through.

If the participant gets frustrated or loses interest in performing the skills, give two to three minute breaks between sets to keep them engage.

Pitching

Pitching is the ability to throw a ball towards the home plate. Pitching helps to improve arm strength, throwing accuracy and coordination. There are five types of pitching: fastball, curveball, knuckleball, slider and forkball pitching. The types of pitching is determined on how the ball is gripped; the fundamental skills remain the same.

Here are the step to perform pitching:

1. Participant should stand with their shoulders square, the non-dominant foot in front of their body and the dominant foot behind.
2. Hold the ball in the dominant arm.
3. Step forward with the non-dominant leg, rotate the hips and shoulders into the direction they will throw.
4. Extend the non-dominant arm out from their waist and swing the dominant arm forward to release the ball and follow through once you release the ball.
5. Do three sets of 20 reps, three to five times per week.

Figure 12: Proper way to hold a baseball

Adaptive Pitching (Hands on technique)

1. Demonstrate visually how to perform all the steps above for the participant to observe.

2. Assist the participant with positioning their body with their shoulders squared, knees slightly bent, the non-dominant foot in front of their body, and the dominant foot behind their body.

3. Stand behind the participant to assist them with stepping forward with non-dominant foot.

4. Assist the participant with rotating their hips and shoulders in the direction they are throwing the ball.

5. Hold their lower arm between the elbows and assist them with extending the dominant arm to release the ball and follow through.

6. Do three set of 15 reps, three to five times per week.

If the participant gets frustrated or loses interest in performing the skills, give two to three minute breaks between sets to keep them engaged.

Catching

Catching is the ability to secure possession of the baseball from the air and maintain full possession. Players use baseball gloves or baseball mittens to catch.

Catching helps to improve eye-hand coordination, visual spatial awareness, and tracking skill. Here are the steps to perform catching a baseball:

Catching the baseball

1. Participant should first put on the baseball glove on the non-dominant hand.
2. Stand with feet apart and knees slightly bent facing the pitcher.
3. Place baseball glove at the center of their body between their shoulders.
4. Position the catching hand into an upright position with fingers pointing up and wrist slightly flexed backward; keep the other hand facing the side of the catching hand.
5. Position the body in front of the ball, then extend the arm forward in the direction of the oncoming ball, then catch the ball
6. Do three sets of 20 reps, three to five times per week

Figure 13: Proper way to catch a baseball

Hands on Technique for catching baseball

1. Visually demonstrate how to perform the skills so that the participant can observe it.

2. Assist the participant with putting on their gloves on the non-dominant hand.

3. Place two poly spots on the ground five inches apart for the participant to stand on, with knees slightly bent.

4. Assist the participants with positioning their catching hand in the center of their body, between

both shoulders, with their wrist flexed backward and finger pointing up (hand in hi-five position).

5. The other hand should be facing the side of the catching hand.

6. Stand behind the participant and place your hands over the participant's lower arm to assist with extending their arms forward to catch the ball.

7. Do three sets of 15 reps, three to five times per week.

If the participant gets frustrated or loses interest in performing the skills, give two to three minute breaks between sets to keep them engaged.

Chapter 5

BADMINTON

Safety Precautions:

❖ Participants should be wearing the appreciate clothing, gloves and shoes. I recommend tennis shoes with ankles support and sufficient support at the bottom to avoid knees and shin splints injuries.

❖ Gloves will help with hands inflation especially if you are playing for long period.

❖ Wear eyes protection such as badminton glass to avoid eyes injuries.

❖ Participant should warm up for 10 minutes and do some stretching.

❖ Badminton drills should be performed in open space. I recommend basketball ball court or big gymnasium.

Check the surrounding area to make sure it is safe. Avoid wet court and debris. This will minimize sliding injuries.

❖ Use the correct size badminton racket. The size and weight of the racket is based on the participant's age.

❖ Instructor/Parents should ensure that the participant performs the skills the correct way.

❖ Participants should bend their arm when swinging the bat.

❖ Avoid too many power swing, this can cause muscles injuries.

Rules:

❖ Badminton is an individual and a team sport.

❖ A match consists of three sets (games) of 21 points

❖ Player/team is awarded a point when the player successfully hits the shuttlecock over the net and it hits the ground or if the opposing team tries to return the shuttlecock and it hits the net.

❖ Players have one chance to get the shuttlecock over the net when serving.

❖ Players are not allowed to touch the net with their racket- this is a foul.

❖ If there is a tie of the games, there is sudden death and the game continues, a team needs to win by two points.

Badminton is a team and individual sport that is played with a shuttlecock, tall net and rackets. Badminton helps to improve eye-hand coordination, tracking and visually spatial awareness. The fundamental skills needed to play badminton are: forehand, backhand, and serving.

Forehand

Here are the steps to perform forehand hitting:

1. Participant should stand with feet apart, both leg shoulder width

2. Hold the racket firmly in the dominant hand and position the arm in an upright position slightly above the shoulder.

3. Step forward with the non-dominant leg and slightly rotate the shoulder and hips in the direction of the oncoming shuttlecock (birdie); as they swing their arm forward to make contact with shuttlecock, and follow through.

4. Do three sets of 20 reps, three to five times per week.

Figure 14: Proper way to hold the badminton racket for forehand batting

Adaptive Forehand (Hands on Technique)

1. Demonstrate visually how to perform the skills for the participant to observe.

2. Place three poly spots in a triangle approximately five inches apart for the participant to stand on and step onto.

3. Assist the participant with standing on two poly spots with feet apart.

4. Assist them with holding the racket with both hands with a firm grip, positioned across the chest and slightly above the shoulder.

5. Stand behind the participant holding the lower part of

6. His/her dominant arm, between the elbow and wrist.

7. Assist the participant with stepping forward with the non-dominant leg and with rotating the shoulder and hips in the direction of the oncoming shuttlecock. And holding their arm, assist them with swinging their arm forward to make contact with shuttlecock, and follow through.

8. Do three sets of 20 reps, three to five times per week.

Backhand

Steps needed to perform backhand are:

1. Participant should stand sideways, with their feet apart at shoulder width and their knees bent.

2. Holding the racket in the dominant arm, position the arm across the chest and above the shoulder.

3. Step forward with the dominant leg and rotate the shoulder and hips as they swing their arm in the direction of the oncoming shuttlecock to make contact, then follow through.

4. Do three sets of 20 reps, three to five times per week

Figure 15: Proper way to hold the badminton racket for backhand batting

Adaptive Backhand (Hand on Technique)

Steps for performing hand on technique for backhand are:

1. Demonstrate visually how to perform the skills for the participant to observe.
2. Place three poly spots in line approximately five inches apart for the participant to stand on and step onto.
3. Assist the participant with standing sideways, with their feet apart at shoulder width and their knees bent. The non-dominant leg should be on the middle poly spot and the dominant leg should be on the back poly spot.
4. Stand behind the participants holding the lower part of their dominant arms between elbows and wrists, as they hold the racket with a firm grip.
5. Assist them in positioning the arm across the chest and above the shoulder.
6. Have the participants step forward with the dominant legs and assist them in rotating their shoulders and hips as you help them to swing their arm in the direction of the oncoming shuttlecock to make contact, then follow through.

7. Do three sets of 20 reps, three to five times per week.

Serving

The steps for serving a shuttlecock:

1. The participant should stand sideways with feet apart shoulder width and knees slightly bent.

2. Hold the shuttlecock in the non-dominant hand and the racket with the dominant hand in an upright position and elbows bent.

3. Rotate the shoulders and hip as they toss the shuttlecock eight (8) to ten (10) inches in the air, and just after it changes direction and begins to fall back down; swing their arms with the racket to make contact with the shuttlecock, and follow through.

4. Do three sets of 20 reps, three to five times per week.

Figure 16: Proper form for serving in badminton

Adaptive serving techniques for Badminton

1. Demonstrate visually how to perform the skills for the participant to observe.

2. Place three poly spots in line approximately five inches apart for the participant to stand on and step onto.

3. Assist the participant with standing sideways, with their feet apart at shoulder width and their knees bent. The non-dominant leg should

be on the middle poly spot and the dominant leg should be on the back poly spot.

4. Place the shuttlecock in the participants non-dominant hand and the racket with the dominant hand in an upright position and elbows bent.

8. Stand behind the participant holding the lower part of both arms, between elbow and wrist, as they hold the racket with a firm grip.

5. Assist them with Rotating their shoulders and hip and tossing the shuttlecock eight (8) to ten (10) inches in the air, and just after it changes direction and begins to fall back down, swing their arm with the racket to make contact with the shuttlecock, and follow through.

6. Do three sets of 20 reps, three to five times per week.

Chapter 6

TENNIS

Safety Precautions:

- ❖ Perform basic warm ups and stretching to loosen your muscles.
- ❖ Use proper safety equipment such as: correct size tennis racket, tennis shoes, comfortable tennis shorts and shirt.
- ❖ Participant should use an age appropriate size racket to minimize injuries.
- ❖ Skill should be performed in an open space example tennis court.
- ❖ Check the court first for cracks and wet spots to minimize injuries.
- ❖ Use correct form to prevent injuries such as: keeping the arms bend when they hit the balls to minimize shoulder injuries.

Rules:

- ❖ Equipment used: Tennis racket, tennis ball.
- ❖ Point are awarded in 15, 30, 40 and game point. If the game is tied 40-40 it's a deuce and the player

needs to win two consecutive points to win the game.

❖ A set comprises six games. Player must win six games to win a set. If there is a tie, then they go to sudden death and a player must win by getting two consecutive points.

❖ For females, it's the best of three sets to win the match and for males its best of five sets to win the match.

❖ When serving, players should alternate the sides they are serving.

❖ If a player touches the net or distracts the other player, they lose points.

❖ If the player hits the ball into the net or outside of the tennis court area they lose points.

Tennis can be played as a team or individual sport. In an individual match there are two players playing against each other; and in a team match there are four players with two players on each team. The object of the game is to successfully hit the ball over the net and the ball must land inside the lines. Tennis helps to improve eye-hand coordination, tracking and visually spatial awareness.

There are three fundamental skills in tennis: forehand, backhand and serving.

Tennis Forehand

The steps for forehand are:

1. Stand facing the net with feet five inches apart, knees bent, and body slightly leaning forward.
2. Hold the racket with the dominant hand between center of shoulders and below the waist.
3. As the ball approaches, step forward with the non-dominant leg and position the dominant arm upright with elbows bent as they rotate the shoulder and hip in the direction of the ball and swing the racket across their body to make contact with ball and follow through.
4. Do three sets of 20 reps, three to five times per week

Figure 17: Proper way to hold the tennis racket for forehand

Adaptive Tennis Forehand (Hands on Technique)

1. Demonstrate visually all the steps to perform the skills for the participant to observe.
2. Place three poly spots on the ground in the shape of an "L". Two for the participant to stand on and one to step on.
3. Assist the participant with standing on two poly spots facing the net with feet five inches

apart, knees bent, and body slightly leaning forward.

4. Place the racket in their dominant hand between the center of shoulders and below the waist.

5. Stand behind the participant holding their lower arm slightly above the wrist. As the ball approaches, assist the participant with stepping forward with the non-dominant leg and positioning the dominant arm upright with elbows bent as they rotate the hip in the direction of the ball and assist them with swinging the racket across their body to make contact with ball, and follow through.

6. Do three sets of 20 reps, three to five times per week.

Tennis Backhand

Steps to perform backhand on tennis are:

1. Stand facing the net with feet five inches apart, knees bent, and body slightly leaning forward.

2. Hold the racket with both hands for better control, between center of shoulders and below the waist.

3. Position the racket across the chest towards the non-dominant side.

4. As the ball approaches, step forward with the dominant leg and swing the racket from the non-dominant side rotate the shoulder and hip in the direction of the ball and swing the racket across their body to make contact with ball and follow through.

5. Do three sets of 20 reps, three to five times per week.

Figure 18: Proper way to hold the tennis racket for backhand

Adaptive Backhand (Hand on technique)

1. Demonstrate visually all the steps to perform the skills for the participant to observe.

2. Place three poly spots on the ground in the shape of an "L". Two for the participant to stand on and one to step on.

3. Assist the participant with standing on two poly spots facing the net with feet five inches apart, knees bent, and body slightly leaning forward.

4. Place the racket in their dominant hand between center of shoulders and below the waist.

5. Stand behind the participant holding their lower arm slightly above the waist

6. As the ball approaches, assist the participant with stepping forward with the dominant leg, rotating the shoulder and hip in the direction of the ball and assist them with swinging the racket across their body to make contact with ball, and follow through.

7. Do three sets of 20 reps, three to five times per week.

Tennis Serving

1. The participant should stand sideways with feet apart at shoulder width and knees slightly bent.
2. Hold the tennis ball in the non-dominant hand with a firm grip and the racket in the dominant hand in an upright position and elbows bent.
3. Rotate the shoulders and hip as they toss the ball four (4) to six (6) inches in the air, and just after it changes direction and begins to fall back down; swing their arms with the racket to make contact with the ball, and follow through.
4. Do three sets of 20 reps, three to five times per week.

Figure 19: Proper form for serving in tennis

Adaptive Serving techniques for Tennis

1. Demonstrate visually how to perform the skills for the participant to observe.

2. Place three poly spots in line approximately five inches apart for the participant to stand on and step on to.

3. Assist the participant with standing sideways, with their feet apart at shoulder width and their knees bent. The non-dominant leg should be on the middle poly spot and the dominant leg should be on the back poly spot.

4. Place the tennis ball in the participants non-dominant hand and the racket in the dominant hand in an upright position with elbows bent.

9. Stand behind the participant holding the lower part of both arms, between elbow and wrist, as they hold the racket with a firm grip.

5. Assist them with rotating their shoulders and hip and tossing the ball four (4) to six (6) inches in the air, and just after it changes direction and begins to fall back down swing their arm with the racket to make contact with the ball, and follow through.

6. Do three sets of 20 reps, three to five times per week.

Chapter 7

TRACK

Safety Precaution:

- ❖ Participant should wear the correct track and field gears such as proper running shoes, running shorts/tights and shirt.
- ❖ Drills should be performed on grass or at a track field to minimize injuries.
- ❖ Participant should warm up for 10 minutes, so as to stretch muscles before starting activities.
- ❖ Use the correct form at all times when performing the drill to avoid injuries.

Rules:

- ❖ When running sprints (100m, 200m and 400m), runners MUST stay on their lanes or they will be disqualified. When running long distance after the first 100m, they can run in any lane.
- ❖ Runners are only allowed to have one false start
- ❖ Runners cannot trip or push anyone

Track is a sport that involves running. It can be a team sport or an individual sport. Track events include: sprinting, middle distance and long distance. These events are performed indoor or outdoor. Running helps to improve cardio vascular endurance, strength speed, coordination muscle toning, and burning body fat.

There are two types of starting position, they are: standing start and bending start. Standing start is used mostly for middle distance, long distance, cross county, and marathon races. Bending start is used mostly for sprinting events such as: 100 meter, 200 meter and 400 meter races.

Running

Here are the steps to perform running:

1. Participant should stand in position on the ball of their feet with the body slightly leaned forward, the non-dominant leg in front, the dominant leg at the back, and knees and arms bent.
2. Begin running by pushing off from the ball of their feet, driving the arms forward with knees high, body in an upright position and alternating arms

and legs with opposite legs and arms (coordination).

3. Hands should rise to the side of the chin and the other hand should be close to the pocket.

Figure 20: Proper running form

Adapting Running (Hands on Technique)

1. Demonstrate visually how to perform the steps for the participant to observe.

2. Start out with stationary running (running on the spot).

3. Assist the participant to stand in position on the ball of their feet with the body slightly leaned forward, the non-dominant leg in front, the dominant leg at the back, and knees and arms bent.

4. Stand behind the participant and place your hands over both of the participant's lower arm to assist them with alternating arms and leg. As you drive their arm forward (close to the chin), they should drive the opposite leg upward.

5. Once the participant has mastered stationary running, they should practice running in motion.

6. Do three sets of 15 reps, three to five times per week.

Walk slowly for the first few sets, to make sure the participant focuses on their technique, then increase the speed of running once they master the correct form without assistance.

Chapter 8

VOLLEYBALL

Safety Precautions:

❖ Participant should wear the proper safety gears such as volleyball shoes to minimize sliding, light clothing to move freely, knee pads and elbow pads.

❖ Use the correct size of volleyball with the proper inflation.

❖ Warm up for 10 minutes and stretch before performing the skills.

❖ Drills should be performed in an open space on the proper volleyball surface to minimize injuries.

❖ Always check for wet spots and debris.

❖ Minimize collision during games.

❖ Execute skills in the correct way to avoid injuries.

Rules:

❖ There are six players on each team.

❖ Points are awarded when the player hits the ball into the opponent's side of the net and the opponents are unable to successfully return the ball.

❖ There are 25 points in each game and the team must win by two points.

❖ The best out of three games wins the competition.

❖ If the ball touches the ground on your side of the net, the opposing team gets a point.

❖ If the ball hits the net on your side, the opposing team gets a point.

❖ Players can not catch or throw the ball, they cannot double hit the ball as well.

❖ When serving, feet cannot go outside the boundary lines.

❖ Players cannot touch the nets.

Volleyball is a team sport. Each team has 6 players and they are separated by a net. The object of the game is to hit the ball with their hands over the net and to keep the ball from hitting the ground. The two fundamental skills needed to play volleyball are: passing and serving. Volleyball helps to improve eye-hand coordination, tracking, strength and visually spatial awareness.

Passing

1. Participant should stand with feet apart at shoulder width, and knees slightly bent.

2. Position the hands to create a *platform* to hit the ball by opening both palms facing upwards, then placing one hand inside the other, then fold both hands in and close with the thumbs.

3. As the ball approaches, step forward with the non-dominant leg (knees remain bent); and extend arms and knees straight out to hit the ball as hard as possible and follow through with the arms.

4. Do three sets of 20 reps, three to five times per week.

Figure 21: Proper form for passing a volleyball

Hands on techniques for passing Volleyball

1. Visually demonstrate the techniques described above for the participant to observe.

2. Place three poly spots on the ground in shape of a triangle. Two spots to stand on in the ready position and one in front to step into the hit.

3. Assist participant with standing on the poly spot with feet apart at shoulder width, and knees slightly bent.

4. Assist participants with positioning their hands to create a *platform* to hit the ball by opening both palms facing upwards, then placing one hand inside the other, then folding both hands inwards and closing with the thumbs.

5. Stand behind the participant holding both arms between the elbows and the wrist to assist them with hitting the ball.

6. As the ball approaches, assist the participant with stepping forward with the non-dominant leg (knees remain bent); and extending their arms and knees straight out to hit the ball as hard as possible and follow through with arms.

7. Do three sets of 20 reps, three to five times per week.

Serving

Serving is used primarily to start the game. Here are the steps to serve a volleyball:

1. Participant should stand with the non-dominant foot forward facing the net. The dominant foot should be in line with the shoulders.

2. The palms of the non-dominant hand should be facing upwards.

3. Place the ball in the palm, with elbows slightly flexed and arm extended out to the front.

4. Position the dominant hand slightly above the ears with palm open.

5. Extend the non-dominant arm all the way up to toss the ball approximately two feet in the air, in line with the hitting shoulders, as they step forward with the non-dominant leg and extend dominant hand to hit the ball.

6. The dominant hand should make contact with the ball just after it changes direction and begins to fall back down; and the ball should make contact with the heel of the wrist.

7. Do three sets of 15 reps three to five times per week.

Figure 22: Starting position to serve a volleyball

Hands on technique for serving a volleyball

1. Visually demonstrate the techniques described above for the participant to observe.
2. Place three poly spots in line for the participant to stand on.
3. Assist the participant with placing their non-dominant foot on the middle poly spot facing the

net, and the dominant foot on the back poly spot in line with the shoulders.

4. The palms of the non-dominant hand should be facing upwards.

5. Place the ball in the palm, with elbows slightly flexed and arm extended out to the front.

6. Stand behind the participant and assist them with positioning the dominant hand slightly above the ears with the palm open.

7. Hold the participant's hands between the elbow and the wrist to assist them with extending the non-dominant arm all the way up to toss the ball approximately two feet in the air, in line with the hitting shoulders, as they step forward with the non-dominant leg, and assist them with extending the dominant hand to hit the ball as hard as possible.

8. Remember that the dominant hand should make contact with the ball just after it changes direction and begins to fall back down; and the ball should make contact with the heel of the wrist.

9. Do three sets of 15 reps three to five times per week.

Chapter 9

SOFTBALL

Safety Precautions:

❖ All participant should wear proper safety gear such as: the helmet, softball catching gloves, softball cleats, correct size bat and appropriate clothing to play freely.

❖ Parents should use an open space such as a grass field to practice the skills.

❖ Ensure that the surface is clear of all debris. Check for cracks on wet spots. Avoid wet surface to minimize injuries.

❖ Remind the participant to use the proper techniques during drills, for example avoid batting with a straight arm. Also ensure that they rotate their body correctly to prevent injuries.

Rules:

❖ There are nine players on the team and there are seven innings in the game

- ❖ After hitting the ball, the runner must drop the bat to run and the runner must touch the bases
- ❖ The batter is out if they receive three strives, or if the batter bats the ball in the air and it's caught, and if the batter does not return to base before the ball.
- ❖ First base is a single, second base is a double, and third base is a triple and then home run.

Softball is a team sport played between two teams. It's very similar to baseball, however the ball is thrown underhand and the game is played for 7 innings. Softball helps to develop coordination, arm strength and eye-hand coordination. There are three fundamental skills needed to play softball, they are: batting, pitching and catching.

Pitching a softball

Here are the steps to perform pitching softball:

1. Participant should stand sideways with legs apart, the non-dominant leg in front of their body and the dominant leg behind, and both arms extended.
2. The ball should be in the dominant hand extended upward to the back and the other hand should be extended forward.

3. Step forward with the non-dominant leg as they rotate their arm into a circular motion as they rotate the hips and shoulders in the direction they are throwing the ball.

4. From the circular motion, extend the arm from their waist and flex their wrist outward to release the ball and follow through.

5. Do three sets of 20 reps, three to four times per week.

Figure 23: Proper form to pitch a softball

Adaptive Softball Pitching

1. Demonstrate visually how to perform all the steps for the participant to observe.
2. Place three poly spots in a line, approximately five inches apart.
3. Participants should stand on two of the poly spots with feet apart and facing sideways.
4. Assist participant with placing their non-dominant leg on the middle poly spot and the other leg on back poly spot.
5. Place the ball in the participant's dominant arm and assist them with extending that arm backwards, and the other arm straight forward.
6. Stand behind the participant to assist them with stepping forward with their non-dominant leg.
7. Hold their lower arm between elbow and wrist to assist the participant with rotating their throwing arms in a circular motion, as they step forward and rotate their hips and shoulders in the direction they are throwing
8. Assist the participant with extending their arm out from their waist, and flex their wrist outward to release the ball, and follow through.
9. Do three set of 15 reps, three to four times per week.
   Batting the Softball
1. The participant should stand sideways with their shoulder squared, feet apart, with the non-dominant leg facing the pitcher and dominant leg behind.
2. Hold the bat tightly with both hands close to each other.

3. Slightly bend their knees.

4. Position the arms (holding the bat) all the way back.

5. Rotate the hips and shoulders and swing the arms forward across the body to make contact with the ball.

6. Follow through across the body after they make contact with ball.

7. Do three set of 20, three to five times per week

Parents or coaches can use their discretion to do more repetitions if the participant is capable of doing so without being fatigued or frustrated.

Batting the Softball

8. The participant should stand sideways with their shoulder squared, feet apart, with the non-dominant leg facing the pitcher and dominant leg behind.

9. Hold the bat tightly with both hands close to each other.

10. Slightly bend their knees.

11. Position the arms (holding the bat) all the way back.

12. Rotate the hips and shoulders and swing the arms forward across the body to make contact with the ball.

13. Follow through across the body after they make contact with ball.

14. Do three set of 20, three to five times per week

Parents or coaches can use their discretion to do more repetitions if the participant is capable of doing so without being fatigued or frustrated.

Figure 24: Starting position to bat a softball

Adaptive Batting

1. Visually demonstrate how to perform all the steps for the participant to observe.

2. Place two poly spots five inches apart from each other.

3. Assist the participant with the proper stance: standing sideways with feet apart, the non-

dominant leg in front and the dominant leg behind.

4. Hold the bat with both hands tightly gripped, and their knees slightly bent.

5. Assist the participant with positioning their arms towards the back.

6. Stand behind the participants placing your hands over their lower arms to assist them with moving their arms forward, swinging the bat as they rotate their shoulder and hips toward the direction of the pitcher.

7. As the bat makes contact with the ball, the participant should follow through.

If the participant gets frustrated or loses interest in performing the skills, give two to three minute breaks between sets to keep them engaged.

Catching a softball

Catching is the ability to secure possession of the baseball from the air and maintain full possession. Players use baseball gloves or baseball mittens to catch. Catching helps to improve eye-hand coordination, visual spatial awareness, and tracking skill. Here are the steps to perform catching a baseball:

1. Participant should first put on the softball glove on the non-dominant hand.
2. Stand with feet apart and knees slightly bent facing the pitcher.
3. Place the softball glove at the center of their body between their shoulders.
4. Position the catching hand into an upright position with fingers pointing up and wrist slightly flexed backward; keep the other hand facing the side of the catching hand.
5. Position the body in front of the ball, then extend the arm forward in the direction of the oncoming ball the catch the ball.
6. Do three sets of 20 reps, three to five times per week.

Hands on Technique for catching a softball

1. Visually demonstrate how to perform the skills so that the participant can observe.

2. Assist the participant with putting on their glove on the non-dominant hand.

3. Place two poly spots on the ground five inches apart for the participant to stand on, with knees slightly bent.

4. Assist the participant with positioning their catching hand in the center of their body, between both shoulders, with their wrist flexed backward and finger pointing up (hand in hi-five position).

5. The other hand should be facing the side of the catching hand.

6. Stand behind the participant and place your hands over the participant's lower arm to assist with extending their arms forward to catch the ball.

7. Do three sets of 15 reps, three to five times per week.

If the participant gets frustrated or loses interest in performing the skills, give a break between sets.